WAMPANOAG ART FOR THE AGES

TRADITIONAL AND TRANSITIONAL

I0759801

By Lee Roscoe

Wampanoag Art for the Ages, Traditional and Transitional

Copyright © 2022 by Lee Roscoe

All rights reserved. No part of this publication may be reproduced, distributed, or transmitted in any form or by any means, including photocopying, recording, or other electronic or mechanical methods, without the prior written permission of the publisher, except in the case of brief quotations embodied in critical reviews and certain other noncommercial uses permitted by copyright law.

ISBN 978-0-578-26292-5
eBook - ISBN 978-0-578-26293-2

Published by
Coyote Press
Post Office Box 188
Orleans MA 02653

Ordering Information: info@artistsandmusicians.org

Website https://www.artistsandmusicians.org/wampanoag

Subject: Indigenous Arts and Crafts

Printed in the United States of America

Book design: Lee Roscoe and Paraclete Press

Cover Art:

TOP ROW, LEFT TO RIGHT: Matting by Leah Llanes (Photo by Leah Llanes, see page 15); *Wetu* built by Jonathan Perry (Photo by Elizabeth James Perry, see page 5); *Eninougby* Julia Marden (Photo courtesy of the artist, see page 41). ***BOTTOM ROW, LEFT TO RIGHT:*** Twined bag by Julia Marden (Photo courtesy of the artist, see page 18); Wampum belt by Elizabeth James Perry (Photo by Elizabeth James Perry, see page 28); Breechclout and leggings by Anita Peters (Photo courtesy of the artist, see page 44); *The First Round* by Robert Peters (Photo courtesy of the artist, see page 54). ***BACK COVER:*** *The Honor Beat*, by Robert Peters (Photo courtesy of the artist)

With honor to the Wampanoag nation (whose name means People of the First Light) and the tribal members in this text. And with respect and admiration for those who dwell in this land and have done so for hundreds of generations in reciprocity with each other and with the earth, seas, skies, rocks and beings, that future generations may be inspired to learn from them a better way.

With gratitude to G. Thomas Ryan, who produced and enabled this book.

With thanks also to Ramona Peters, and Paula Peters, and to the artists I interviewed. Any mistakes are mine.

Thank you also to Rob Kluin and Richard Pickering of Plimoth Patuxet Museums, and to Ed Maroney, Janet Murphy Robertson, and Bruce Henry.

Contents

1.*Wetu* **interior at Plimoth Patuxet Museums with Philip Wynne Many Hands** (Photo by Richard Taylor)

Foreword

Using their bodies and hands in season to provide for a self-sufficient life, the Wampanoag (as with all indigenous cultures) turn nature into artifacts for needs, some essential, some less so—food, shelter, clothing, warmth—adornment, entertainment, and most importantly ceremony. But there is a thin line between use and ceremony, for the objects which tribespeople crafted and still craft combine the material with the spiritual.

While ceremonial objects were and are created in and of themselves, more quotidian objects, such as a cedar flute or simple eating bowl carved from a burl, could express the sacred (in these cases a thankfulness to the spirit within the tree and the wood), because as Wampanoag elders will tell you, there is always reciprocity between human beings themselves, and between human beings and animals, plants, the whole earth and universe, between what you are taking and what you are giving back.

The year 2020 marked the 400th year of colonization by English Separatists from the Church of England of what would become Massachusetts. They settled in Plymouth, at the native Wampanoag town of Patuxet (also named Apaum and Accomack in early texts), which had been decimated by disease brought down the coast by European fishers, sailors, slavers and explorers, and was described by one 17th century writer as a "Golgotha."

In many ways the English invasion set the trajectory for the American project. Colonization disturbed almost 12,000 years of native life, disrupting it with disease, trade for profit, currency, settled agriculture, Christianity's guilt and the Biblical ethos of dominance over the earth.

This Settler attitude (and material practice) was an antipode to the Wampanoag loving lifeway of living in community with earth, creatures, plants and each other, rather than driven by material greed for accumulation or ego.

Through these centuries the Wampanoag have persevered; they have adapted to Settler culture, but have also preserved and honored their linked material and spiritual traditions. Nothing represents this more than the artisanship they still practice, keeping evolving traditions alive and taking them steps further.

This booklet will look at a few of the many significant Wampanoag artists through some of their basic traditional creations, and also at some non-traditional practitioners, although all the artists I spoke to talk about a connection to the way life was lived, the need to revivify their culture, to bring the past into the present and future.

2. *Wetu*, built by Marcus Hendricks for the Yarmouth Historical Society.
A detail of ties (usually cedar)
(Photo by Elisabeth Perna)

RIGHT TOP:
3. Longhouse (*nush wetu*) built by Marcus Hendricks for the Yarmouth Historical Society (Photo by Elisabeth Perna)

RIGHT BOTTOM:
4. Longhouse, Fruitlands
(Wiki Commons)

LEFT TOP:

5. *Wetu* exterior, Mashpee.

LEFT MIDDLE:

6. Detail of longhouse structure, Mashpee. Robert Peters helped supervise the construction.

LEFT BOTTOM:

7. Interior longhouse wetu, Mashpee. Robert Peters helped supervise the construction.
(Photos courtesy of Robert Peters)

RIGHT:

8. Robert Peters by longhouse
(Photo by Darius Coombs)

TOP:

9. *Wetu* built by Marcus Hendricks for the Yarmouth Historical Society
(Photo by Elisabeth Perna)

BOTTOM:

10. A spring-summer-early autumn home with cattail mats exterior
(Photo courtesy of Elizabeth James Perry)

11. This *wetu*, a large bark (generally winter style) two-fire home is 30 feet long. It is on the island of Aquinnah, Martha's Vineyard. It was built by Jonathan James Perry in 2009. (Photo courtesy of Elizabeth James Perry)

Wetu

WETU spelled also as *weekuw* and *weetu.*

Words in Wôpanâak from the Wôpanâak Language Reclamation Project (see *Provincetown Arts* Magazine 2020, Roscoe) are understandably proprietary, so the Wampanoag words herein are the generic English version.

12. A Mashantucket Pequot Museum and Research Center village panorama
(Photo courtesy of Mashantucket Pequot Museum and Research Center)

I imagine walking into the woods to a magical, peaceful place where the perfume of pine needles is burnished by the scent of a small cooking fire. Through the season I help to build the wetu in which the fire burns, weave the mats which cover it, create the bed frames and lay furs on them, craft pots, tan and stretch hides, sew clothes and foot coverings, gather fiber to twine carrying baskets. In the evening there are stories of history and of the stars.

For it is in the wetu, the home, that all the arts are encompassed.

Annawon Weeden builds *wetus*, (*wetuash*), Wampanoag dwellings, small and large; teaches native culture; carves artifacts; is an actor; and drums and sings with such as Eastern Sons, a group he helped found. He's a NEFA (New England Foundation for the Arts) Native New England Now grant recipient, and received a Congressional honor as Culture Bearer for the entire New England region in 2016, at Rhode Island's Tomaquag Museum. He worked for years at Plimoth Plantation, now renamed Plimoth Patuxet Museums, and at the Boston Children's Museum Native Voices programs, and has shared his tribal culture with the Smithsonian, Harvard University, National Geographic, and Scholastic.

13. Annawon Weeden and wampum
(Photo by Webb Chappell, WGBH archives)

He grew up on the Narragansett reservation in Charlestown, Rhode Island. His mother is Mashpee Wampanoag, his father, Pequot. He says his upbringing, and the discovery of a post card from the 1970s that shows Annawon's father in front of a lodge in the front yard near a trading post he ran, inspired him to intensify the knowledge and practice of his culture.

At Plimoth Patuxet, Annawon had his first opportunity to build a structure himself. "All the arts I learned there, I fell in love with. Burning out bowls, spoons and *mishoons*." (A *mishoon* is a seagoing canoe, fired and dug out, often from white pine or chestnut.)

"A lot of the spoons I make I just give to friends. Making things with which to serve a friend's family honors the work of creating the object." He's also proud of an ornately carved paddle used on a journey to Martha's Vineyard in 2002. "We took our mishoon from Nobska (the light house in Falmouth) over to the Vineyard in 90 minutes, beating the people who were heading there to greet us!

"No discredit to the artists out there and the media they use, but I hate making something which will just hang on a wall. I like to make useful things. I consider a house, building a home, art."

Twenty years back he helped build the Pequot Village at the Mashantucket Pequot Museum in which still stand *wetus*; drying racks for meat, fish and berries; a watch tower to oversee corn planting; and a palisade wall to surround the village. He's built *wetus* at Falmouth's Waquoit Bay Estuarine Reserve, at Salt Pond Visitor Center, in Eastham, and on commission for whatever schools and other institutions want them.

There are summer and winter *wetus*.

A summer *wetu* is a domed house, about 15 feet across, 12 feet high, built of bent cedar sapling frames. Woven cattail mats cover the exterior frame, and woven bulrush matting, the interior. Accommodating six or eight people of a single family, the home belongs to the woman (through whom the family line is descended). She, her immediate family, as well as her in-laws, live there.

The round shape of the *wetu* represents the womb (or as Marcus Hendricks, wampum artisan and Mashpee Wampanoag cultural historian would say, it is in the shape of expectant mothers' stomachs.)

Annawon loves the circular shape. "It is warmer, circulating air; it is airier, and it prevents abuse to the structure during hurricanes or storm. Roundness reflects nature: gardens are round, puddles, every vegetable, even the earth, sun and moon, as well as nests, dens, and eggs." It is unlike the unnatural "square boxy buildings most people find themselves stuck in all day." He cautions, "The square layouts of houses and towns are unhealthy. Wampanoag villages were laid out according to flow of the stars and lunar patterns; everything flowed."

About the people who brought the squares to these shores, Annawon says, "The Pilgrims were too arrogant, they thought they were superior to everyone. They were elitist. Alhough their civilization had failed in Europe, they failed to try something new," to learn from a lifeway which had lasted 12,000 years in relative peace and without destroying the earth which sustained it. "What were they thinking?" he asks, and hopes we can break the cycle of assault they set in place.

The *wetu* frame's white cedar saplings, supple enough to bend, must be gathered at just the right time in spring. The amount of saplings for the frame (often around 30 to 40) depends on the *wetu's* size. The

14. Fall village (Photo courtesy Institute for American Indian Studies)

green saplings are soaked, and bark stripped off. "Cedar is sweet-scented, insect and rot repellant, long lasting; it's not just suitable, it is ideal, flexible, preserves really well when the bark is off, and the bark itself is cordage" with which to tie the frame (also using dogbane and milkweed rope). Paired saplings are placed into holes at a 45-degree angle, the holes filled with stones, and the bent saplings lashed together at the top.

"To kill things is male; the female task, to give life is what women do. For us that's what broke down the roles. Killing trees to build a house is what men would do." (But roles were not rigid. Generally, women, as the life givers, created that which related to what is alive such as mats for the *wetu*, storage baskets, clothing and cooking pots; men as the life takers crafted such as bows, arrows, arrowheads.)

Each step of preparation of materials is a process of both material and spiritual practice, Annawon stresses. "We have to offer our tobacco, our gift of ceremony in return; anytime we take life we do a ceremony. We must ask permission and give thanks for anything which is taken. We even offer tobacco to our crops. You can't expect nature just to produce without giving back. As native people we have to give back, so when I kill the trees, I offer prayer and raw tobacco. My medicine man instructed me to put tobacco in each of the holes dug to put poles into, also. Not only are we disrupting earth by digging, but we are creating a bond between the pole and the earth," so that the *wetu* is not separate from the earth but one with it. (There is also a typically Wampanoag duality, a subtle male and femaleness to this as well.)

"People were content with just a roof over their heads. It's all we needed. You'd have a small house and small family, only one or two children. Small households could care and provide for one or two kids on land which yielded what was necessary for the family." He adds that political or medicine leaders' individual homes might have hosted more people, hence be larger—accommodating more than one spouse (as some leaders were polygamous)—"raising future leaders."

This family unit *wetu* was the warm weather house, near coastal fields planted for corn, bean and squash, and of course near fresh water. Mashpee Wampanoag elder Nancy Eldredge has written that summer *wetuash* were surrounded by acres of gardens for each family. Praise and thanks occurred at each stage of the planting and harvesting, especially with a ceremony for the Green Corn. There were daily prayers to the Dawn, out the eastern door where life begins.

In winter extended families in their matriarchal clans would go farther inland to more hospitable sheltered, forested areas by river headlands and lakes.

Annawon comments that winter was the most bountiful time of year: "There was plenty of hunting for thicker furs for clothing and of course for meat, unlike in warmer weather when animals were tending young and meat could be wormy—plus you'd have what was harvested, corn and dried berries—whereas in the warmer months you would be out in the water, getting fish, lobster, clams, tending crops, cooking, and even sleeping outdoors."

Darius Coombs, formerly the director of Wampanoag and Algonquian Interpretive Training at Plimoth Patuxet Museums and now the Cultural and Outreach Coordinator for Education for the Mashpee Wampanoag, informed me that before Contact, villages housed from 200 to 2,000 people.

Winter villages were communal gatherings of longhouses with domed roofs of up to 150, even 200, feet, Coombs says, with a fire every ten feet for each family grouping, housing up to 20 families, related matrilineally to a common female ancestor. (In all *wetus*, there were bark smoke flaps manipulable from the inside, to protect from the elements and to vent smoke.) A typical *Nush wetu* is a three-fire house (about 30 feet long by 20 feet wide by 12 feet high). Winter longhouses could also be ceremonial, meeting houses, or leadership houses separate from living quarters, according to Aquinnah Wampanoag cultural historian and *wetu* builder Jonathan Perry.

While Annawon can create a single summer *wetu* himself, usually it is a group effort of three or four men, especially for the

15. White cedar (Photo by Lee Roscoe)

winter longhouses. Winter homes might take as many as 200 saplings, and were covered with big sheets of bark, that, before Contact, were of chestnut or elm collected by women. They could be old growth and thus many inches thick. Sadly, these trees have been extincted by blights.

The winter house is shingled with the bark from bottom to top, attached to an exterior frame which serves as a ladder to reach the top. Constructing a 30 foot-long *wetu* can take three weeks. Creating the house from processing the saplings to building to furnishing, including mats, can take three months, Coombs says.

The *wetu* structure is also a reminder of the spiritual beliefs of the people. "Double arches create the eastern door where all things start, are aligned; if there were another it would be at the southwest, because that's where spirit is trying to get to, having started in the east," Annawon explains.

I ask about the pattern of four at the top of a summer *wetu*: is there a connection between four winds, four cardinal directions, and does that connect to major *manitous* or belief figures, culture heroes, and does that in turn connect to the cycle of life, and to the cycle from dawn to dusk and cycle of the seasons?

"Yes, the number four is a sacred number, symbolic of all those if not more," Annawon responds. "For some of us, the sacred number is six."

One of the places Annawon has harvested cedars is the Hockomock swamp in Bridgewater, Raynham, and Taunton. Atlantic white cedar is found only in a hundred-mile strip of the Atlantic and Gulf coasts. With their grey striated trunks and tatting-like evergreen foliage, they create silence, mystery, mist and spookiness. They once grew more prolifically in swamps alongside the rivers of southeastern Massachusetts, until they were cut to drain swamps, to get rid of wolves and especially for cranberry farming in the mid-19th century.

Trees may be hundreds, even thousands of years old and sometimes are named by natives as the tree of life. The acidic waters which house the trees' roots create anaerobic conditions inhospitable to all but a few other species. It is said that cedar swamps were areas into which many Wampanoag fled when threatened by enemies, including the Pilgrims in 1627 after Myles Standish prosecuted a deadly incursion against them.

Evergreens, including cedar, are sacred to the Wampanoag, as part of Creation. Perry says, "They protect us in winter. They watch over creation when everything sleeps," explaining that human beings were originally made of stone, but misunderstood death and so did not respect life. They were then created of wood, the symbology reminding them that they were part of the earth even as the forests were.

Annawon is concerned about conserving, not over-harvesting trees. "Cedar swamps where we harvest, they get choked out. As native people we've always upkept our land, we've maintained it. If you don't remove fallen cedars you have a stand of dead cedar, also cedar need controlled burns. It is the only way, as far as I know, to create new ones. I don't hit the same swamp over and over again till it's depleted. Luckily we have a lot of resources and they haven't been completely destroyed."

FACING PAGE:
16. Putting up mats
(Courtesy Elizabeth James Perry. Photo by Jonathan Perry)

Matting

Annawon suggests a newly married couple might have crafted a whole *wetu* together. But ordinarily while men often built the structure out of cedar saplings, women were tasked with the creation of the *wetu* mats, made of cattails for the exterior of the structure, bulrushes, and sometimes cedar for the interior. (Matting was also used for sleeping, drying food, and even carrying infants.)

Mourt's Relation (likely authored by Edward Winslow) wrote of a *wetu* sighted in 1620 on the Outer Cape, "the doore was not over a yard high made of a matt to open... Round about the fire they lay on matts which are their beds...Their houses were double matted." {N.B. Winslow was a leader of the Separatists who came to Plymouth along with those "Strangers" not of their religious persuasion. In spite of other of his henchmen, for decades he maintained excellent relations with the Wampanoag, also known as Pokanoket in old texts, and was Plymouth's governor on occasion.}

Julia Marden is a master mat-maker and twiner. She is an Aquinnah Wampanoag who grew up in Falmouth, summering on the Vineyard, and now lives in Vermont, where her twining and many other arts are available through Bluejay's Vision.

Her work is museum quality, exhibited at the Mashantucket Pequot museum, University of Rhode Island, the Wisconsin Museum of Quilts and Fiber Arts, the Mt. Kearsage Indian Museum, and The Robbins Museum of Archaeology.

For matting, "cattails and bulrushes are usually harvested in late summer, early fall, when the plants are dying and the seed is falling, whereas bark would be collected in early spring when it is supple," Marden says. Dye to color the interior mats was gathered from plants in various times when they were in season. "We followed a natural time clock."

She agrees with Annawon that it is a "tough and tender process," time consuming, to harvest, process and create the mats.

If you've ever tried to tramp through cattail and bulrush wetlands, or harvest cattails for food (young leaves raw, and baby "sausages" cooked, as well as pollen flour and young inner stems), you know how tightly knit the plants are, how defensive—almost aggressively closing in against you. As they should, for they, too, are a diminishing resource due to draining of wetlands and pollution. Cattails like clean water to grow in.

Marden says, "It's harder and harder to get materials, because plants are being squeezed out by invasive species like phragmites. Because of the values, and rules of self-governance we had, we never over-harvested. We would not take the first plants we saw," in order to be sure that they would remain for ongoing generations.

After harvest, cattail leaves are separated from the plant, dried; bulrush 4 to 5 feet long is boiled, then dried. Using a square frame of saplings, the top edge of the cattail mat would be woven, Marden says. (Both bulrush

FACING PAGE TOP :

17. Finished bulrush mat (Courtesy of Leah Llanes and Julia Marden. Photo by Leah Llanes)

FACING PAGE BOTTOM:

18 a, b, c. Bulrush mats in process created by Leah Llanes (Photos by Leah Llanes)

17

18 a

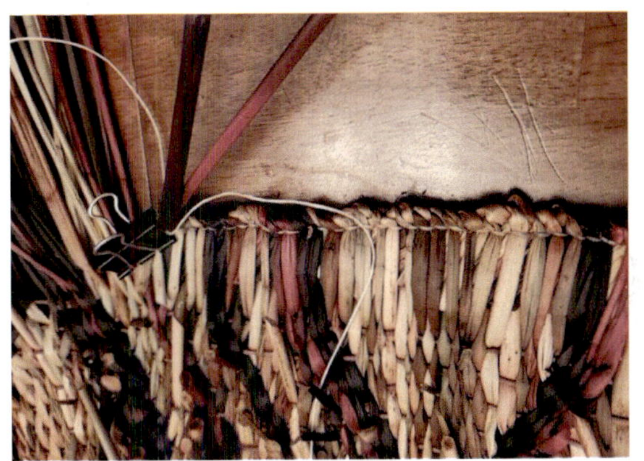

18 b

18 c

and cattail mats are hung, but the selvage is different for each.) Using needles made from deer ribs, cattails would be twisted and sewn in two layers. For a bulrush mat, bulrush warps are interwoven with cordage weft. And with cedar, the inner and outer bark are separated. Then the inner bark is boiled to get the sap out. Divided into pieces, the bark is then woven by plaiting.

Creating a single cattail mat can take a week or less but of course you need multiple mats, some 28 of ten-foot-long cattail mats, according to Darius Coombs. A single bulrush mat, depending on size, takes at least two to three 40-hour work weeks.

Interior rush mats were both decorative, crafted with elaborate designs, and functional, distributing heat rising from the central fire, through the gap of inches between interior and exterior coverings, back down into the *wetu*, even as the smoke rose up through the smoke hole, Marden explains.

The exterior cattail mats "are extremely efficient. Rain runs down the reeds, works into the mats and spins back out." Cattail mats also shrink and dry to let the breeze through in hot weather. Indeed, colonists spoke of *wetus* being much warmer than their own drafty, square houses. "I've been in *wetus* in November while it's freezing outside, and inside I'm sweating," Marden says. "We came up from the Southwest to here, where we have been for 12,000 years. We know how to be comfy, how to create our needs, with intent in design and function."

{For a wonderful account of Chippewa (a related Algonquian speaking tribe) mat weaving, see the Bureau of Ethnology Bulletin 186.}

FACING PAGE

19. Large twined storage bag 2003, commercial hemp and dye 18-20 inches high, created by Julia Marden (Photo courtesy of the artist)

Twining

Twining, according to Julia Marden, is one of the oldest forms of indigenous artisanship wherever there was plant fiber. Twining twists more than one strand of weft around one or more warps, using your fingers and no loom. The warps can be attached to a tree branch, or you can lay fibers out flat on your lap using a cross pattern of strands.

She has been doing it for almost three decades, creating cylindrical and rectangular bags, baskets, quivers, and flat objects, too, such as belts and straps. Recently Marden has crafted a traditional turkey feather mantle completely woven (no feathers are stitched on), "probably the first one in 400 years," she says.

TOP LEFT:

20. Dawn Land Designs closed twine bag with pokeweed dye by Kerri Anne Helme
(Photo courtesy of the artist)

MIDDLE:

21. Horseshoe crab basket, created by Julia Marden and family
(Photo courtesy of Marden)

BOTTOM:

22. Museum-quality twined bags by Julia Marden at Aptuxcet Trading Post event
(Photo by Neil Silberblatt)

TOP RIGHT:

23. Three Generations: Julia Marden with granddaughter Hallee Llanes,who created the twined bag. (Photo by Hallee's mother and Julia's daughter, Leah Llanes)

TOP:
24. Twined fish themed basket by Julia Marden
(Photos courtesy of the artist)

BOTTOM:
25. Twined turkey feather mantle by Julia Marden
(Photo courtesy of the artist)

Marden learned twining at Plimoth Patuxet Museums where she "really took to it." She says (mirroring the other artists I spoke with), "As a contemporary person living now, being able to do what I do is an honor; it connects me directly to my ancestors. And I give thanks to them for their incredible knowledge and incredible art." And she's thankful to pass on the know-how to her daughter Leah Llanes, who created her own unique method of twining a flat bag at the age of seven. And now Julia's 14-year-old granddaughter, Hallee, twines!

When Julia twines a commercial bag, it can take two months of 40-hour weeks, and that's using commercial cordage of hemp, jute or cotton. She makes traditional bags as well (they cost in the thousands to purchase).

Fiber for traditional twining (and weft for some matting) is made of cattails, bulrushes, cornhusks, false nettle, butterfly weed, milkweed, dogbane, and the inner bark of basswood and cedar. Fibers are rubbed in strands of two on a thigh, until they're spun long enough to use. They can be dyed using such as bloodroot, staghorn sumac, walnut or chestnut husks, to colors including yellow, orange, red, black, and brown. The natural color of the fiber is used too.

Twine designs were and are geometric, floral, of the four directions, and the sacred tree of life, Marden says. She also practices an ancient form of twine design: porcupine quill or moose hair wrapped around the fiber cord.

"We made cordage as fine as silk and as heavy as rope for any need you can think of, fishing nets and lines, lashings for houses, as well as storage mats and bags."

Bags in the past were often used to store dried berries, meat, fish and squash, corn and corn flour, seeds, and nuts. "They were 17th century Tupperware. Both artful and beautiful, many were buried in the ground. We lived in summer homes when we planted. We kept our planting seed on site, in storage pits dug below the frost line and lined with mats, in storage bags which held four to six bushels." (Exactly what the colonizers plundered in November of 1620 on Cape Cod at Corn Hill, and later in some part made restitution for.)

There were also twined hulling bags (used to shake off the corn to release the hull), and twined grapevine baskets for clamming, loose-woven so the clams could be rinsed easily. Some artifacts such as belts, garters, ceremonial bags, and pouches were and are made to convey spiritual energy, and may adorn regalia.

Marden also creates dolls, *Eninuog*, the People, wearing the regalia they would have worn at Contact. She and her family, perhaps for the first time in hundreds of years, have created horseshoe crab baskets: Two horseshoe crab shells attached and hung with a twined strap.

Mourt's Relation reports that the colonists exploring the outer Cape saw, "Hand-baskets made of crab-shells wrought together" and "baskets of sundry sorts, bigger and some lesser, finer and some coarser: some were curiously wrought in blacke and white with pretie workes."

These horseshoe crab baskets were not just practical but carried the power of the mystery of the ancient animal in them, known for its emergence under spring full moons to mate and lay eggs into the sand, and then to retreat elusively back under the waters.

"It could take a family to create a basket, storage bag or a mat, learning over a lifetime until you were proficient. Children, adults, elders might work on various segments: gather the plants needed for fiber, process them into cordage, then work on a bag," Marden says, reminding us that creation was communal, twining families together to each other and to the natural world.

26. *Eninuog* doll by Julia Marden 18 inches 2017 wearing prototype miniature twined turkey feather mantle
(Photo courtesy of the artist)

Finger weaving, which apparently started in the 1700s with the arrival of trade wool, is not to be confused with twining. Finger weaving is the art of creating flat material for straps, sashes and leg garters, often with chevron, diamond or lightning designs, by braiding fibers, combining warp and weft, using no loom, but attaching strands to a tree or stick.

Mashpee Wampanoag, Marlene Lopez, in a film for the Smithsonian's National Museum of the American Indian, says the design significance in finger weaving is that there is a center eye, which is creation watching. The strands bring individuals together to create community. The energy and prayers of the maker go into the sash or belt for protection of the wearer. The weaving has continuity for it may be passed down to generations. The fringe (on the ends of the belt or sash, or indeed, Lopez says, any garment) may both sweep the ground, making contact with earth, and, moving with air, bring prayer up to the Creator.

27. Dawn Land Designs, finger weaving of sash in progress, by Kerri Anne Helme
(Photo courtesy of the artist)

28. Finger weaving by Elizabeth James Perry
(Photo courtesy of the artist)

FACING PAGE
29. *The Conversation*, pottery and mise en scene by Ramona Peters (Photo by Ramona Peters)

Pottery

The first colonists invading near the Pamet River in Truro 400 years ago saw wooden bowls, trays, dishes, and earthen pots inside *wetus*. Indeed, pottery for cooking and occasionally for storage of food and water is one of the most ancient arts, in the Americas some 4,800 years old. It may have been discovered when people put clay-covered twined baskets over cooking fires, and they baked into containers.

Revered Bear clan elder, Ramona Peters, Nosapocket, retired recently from eight years as the Mashpee Wampanoag Tribal Historic Preservation Officer where she was also tasked with curating the Mashpee Wampanoag Museum, as well as the tribe's archives. After years of varied service to her people, including acting as one of seven traditional Chief's Councilors, she has returned to her passion for pot making, helping to revive the art of Wampanoag ceramics.

30. Ramona Peters (Photo by David Bernie, courtesy of Ramona Peters)

She's taught all kinds of classes on pottery and her culture, from students at Harvard University, and famous prep schools, to her own people. She's received numerous awards from across the nation for her work in cultural preservation, such as The Mashpee Wampanoag Tribe and The First People's Fund, Community Spirit Award.

Her pots each have a spirit, and are a bit like children, especially vital when she is creating them, although she may forget where they have gone once they have been fired and sent out into the world.

She loved to fashion artifacts from her Wampanoag tribe's past, but it wasn't until she was asked by Plimoth Patuxet Museums to recreate a 17th century vessel that she fell in love specifically with pottery. She basically taught herself the art. "My family has had pieces of ceramics, though we don't know how old they are," which she examined along with museum collections to figure out techniques. "There were styluses to indent or emboss, or paddles with cords wrapped around them to press into wet clay.

"Pots that I make are culturally informed by my Wampanoag ancestors. The shape is traditional, with rounded bottoms which receive heat differently than flat bottomed; the heat is distributed in a circle." These fit onto three large stones, where they perch, held without rocking as the water boils, by incisions carved into them. She adds (echoing Annawon) that "we didn't have square shapes in our culture. Shapes were lines or circles, curves, or spirals."

She says fire goes around a piece of wood and the pot mimics the fire's shape. "There is a body, a collar, neck and head" to her pots, although she notes that some ancient pots did not have necks.

There are male and female elements within a pot which express a "symbolic representation of the way we were, and the way we are."

There are four points on the pot, at the top. "The function is complemented by philosophy, by cosmology; how we behave in the world. The four have many meanings, men going in four directions to bring back food and knowledge to add to the pot. More linear designs on the pot reflect maleness. Males want to get from point A to point B, especially when they are hunting." Female thought, she says, is more nuanced. "The bottom of the pot is female, holding nourishment from nature. The female bottom designs (she calls them tattoos) are more fluid."

Her pieces vary in size from heights of eleven inches to twenty or so, from one-gallon cooking pots to commissioned pots of five or more gallons. Some are shaped like owls, some have lines on them which represent water, some have thunderbirds represented by paired chevrons. Her signature can be found on the upper left corners.

31. Pot by Kerri Helme (Photo courtesy of the artist)

Peters connects with earth, air, fire and water through the clay. The clay collected is "powerful emotionally" in that it "holds so much; it holds lakes and ponds in place. It's a layer of fine earth that's moved so much that the grains are tiny and tight." The minerals combined "are the strongest part of the pot. And then, with earth and water, there are the elementals of fire and air which complete the pot. There's also how the clay you build reacts differently to fire and air."

(Artisan Jonathan Perry points out, "Where clay meets water is the perfect place to create Life. The combination of water, materials and minerals, the right combination, can create growth and life—so the water and clay is the birth of life," both, he says, in oral tradition and borne out scientifically.)

For a time, friends would leave clay dug from local river banks near Nosapocket's door. Clay on the Cape can be found in dune scarps on the Highlands, and famously on Martha's Vineyard in the colored cliffs of Aquinnah, where a unique pottery was developed in the 19th century and later made famous by Gladys Widdiss and the Vanderhoop family. Ramona both purchases and digs her clay.

No glazes were or are used, but pieces of crushed rocks used by inland tribes and crushed shells used by coastal ones allow pots to go from the high heat of firing to cooling without breakage. Red and yellow ochre and charcoal black was painted on some pieces through the centuries, she adds.

She creates her pots from coil upon coil of clay. "My strongest experience with a pot I make is when the shape is formed but damp enough to carve designs into it. The pot sings. After I fire and dry it, it is done for me."

She fires some pots traditionally in a pit, with brush, but many in her own small kiln. Pots are finished by turning the piece onto its four points as a pedestal to rest while firing the piece inside with horsetail grass filling it. "Pots were used in summertime which were not treated, but left porous so that water would evaporate through and remain cool. Ceramics were also used for pipes, beads and other artifacts."

While most of Nosapocket's pots are used as objects of beauty to appreciate, she reminds us that pots were fully functional, used not only to cook with but for storage of bear grease, whale oil, pigments, water, and even for human ashes as urns during "the period in Wampanoag cultural evolution where mortuary practices included cremation."

She has created pots by commission for private individuals and for many public institutions, such as the Mashantucket Pequot and the Peabody museums, most recently for the permanent collections at The Box Museum in Plymouth, England which features Wampanoag art to commemorate the Plymouth 400th. Her pots have been exhibited throughout the eastern seaboard as well as in Japan, where they were compared to the millennia-old Jomon pottery. As the founder of the Native Land Conservancy, the first of its kind in the East to preserve undeveloped native lands, protect sacred, natural and cultural resources and encourage the continuation of Native American traditional lifeways of the Northeast, she has created pots as gifts for people who've donated land. And she gifts friends, sometimes designing the pot for their cultures, as when she used glyphs from Taino culture for a Taino friend.

But some pots she holds onto. "The Conversation" is a whimsical colloquy of pots resembling animals "talking about what is going on in the natural world. Not just global warming. There's a drastic difference in the natural world than our ancestors, pre-Contact, experienced. On every level, the earth has been changed. We as indigenous people feel that. I need to express it. There's a half circle, a fence behind them (the pots) with a motif on it. The natural world is fenced in. They're having a conversation about it—the restricted habitats. This is the same as with the tribes, what happened to them; limited mobility."

FACING PAGE:
32. Diplomatic Wampum Belt, by Elizabeth James Perry. Thick white wampum disc beads created with electric drill, woven in wildcrafted handspun, hand-dyed milkweed plant fiber, 2019.
(Photo by the artist)

Wampum

While the arts of shelter, twining and pottery always had a ceremonial aspect, no art was more tied into ceremony itself than the creation and use of wampum.

Elizabeth James Perry is an Aquinnah Wampanoag who has a foot in Settler culture as a marine biologist and a foot in native civilization as a museum-exhibited artist. In addition to many fellowships and honors, including the Rebecca Blunk Award for her dedication to Northeastern arts, Perry is a New England Foundation for the Arts grantee. She's exhibited in museums such as the Peabody Essex, and she sells to collectors.

She's worked on native dancers' beaded and quilled moccasins, and on handpainted clothing, combining traditional brain tanned and smoked deerskin with modern acrylic paints for intricate patterns which she presses into the surface (in a process that can take as long as 16 hours). She twines, weaves, crafts clothing, paints, and creates wampum artifacts meticulously by hand.

As a child, she was barely able to get downstairs to the basement where her mum, aunts and cousins would do bead work, but she loved to watch and join in and began doing art early on, creating her first weaving when she was just 8. Perry credits her mother and cousin Helen Haynes and Helen's daughter Helen Attaquin (Ph.D.), author and educator, for teaching her and for passing on the cultural knowledge essential for the founding of Plimoth Patuxet's Wampanoag program.

33. Elizabeth James Perry
(Photo by her brother, Jonathan James Perry)

Whether in Dartmouth where Perry lives now, or on Martha's Vineyard, she says, "We always spent time by the sea, at the beach, clamming, swimming. We canoed the waterways, the inland rivers. I'm descended from whalers. I grew up with those stories. There's always one person in a family interested in the stories, the genealogy, the artifacts, and I'm that person.

"Ocean water is the origin of life. so important to coastal and island people because it defines us. We draw sustenance from it a lot of the year whether lobster, clams, oysters, fishes, or whales, or in the past, sea mink or certain birds; it's a means of major transportation; you could see fleets of *mishoons* heading to visit, fish or trade. It's just a source of life and so much happens out on the ocean." The ocean drew her to marine biology, which gives her a chance to "help to improve the health of the oceans and the creatures in them I love" so it's not all "relentless taking. So we can minimize our impact."

And wampum is also very much of the sea, Perry says, tooled as it is from the quahogs and whelks which also give much loved food to the People. The connection to water as medicine confers great spiritual power to wampum, she says, and "has a lot to do with acknowledging the connection between the sea and sky."

Wampum means white and *peak*, bead. The darker purples were *mooihack(ee),* and *suki hoak*, the lavender. Indeed, Perry says, Suki could be a girl's name, indicating "precious." (It is the makeup of the substrate which the animals live in and what they eat that likely causes the coloration.)

"It has the gorgeous duality of purple ground allied with the white symbolism of sky," Perry says, a "complementary duality" which is an essential part of indigenous belief. "It's not judgmental, not the hard and fast judgment of good and evil, but different aspects of creation." Or, as another source says, "The combination of white and purple represented the duality of the world; light and dark, sun and moon, woman and man, life and death."

Purple may indicate "seriousness, sadness, hardship, tougher times. It's likely to be worn by adults, and white by children because they are new," innocent, Perry explains. White indicates peacefulness, "mindfulness, purity, spiritual insight, diplomacy. The white wampum is the strongest material associated with those ideas along with eagle feathers." Barbara Robinson's *Native American Sourcebook* adds that, "In the symbolism of the northeast white represents Life which is equated with Light, Mind, Knowledge, Great Being, and the continuity of human social life."

Wampum also embodies "a lot of star symbolism ... going back to ancient traditions, observances and celebrations around certain constellations at certain times of year," Perry adds. And it is "about sharing abundance. It has a lot to do with taking care of our ancestors and the next generation," as a reminder of communal engagement, reciprocity—that if you do well, to make sure that others, elders, the young, receive that bounty.

34. E.J. Perry Woven Porcupine Quillwork Man's Bracelet Cuff. Porcupine quill, cotton thread, natural dyes and mordants, smoked deerskin (Photo courtesy of the artist)

"There is a nice steady quality to the traditions and the knowledge-keeping used to cement alliances and agreements which are used to strengthen bonds (between humans and between them and the universe). It's this witnessing material that's present in any important event even today. It is an ancient tradition with a lot of complexity to it. There's a lot of specialized sacred knowledge which is not publicly shared. At its heart it's a very social medium; that's how Algonquian people envisioned it and that's how we deployed it. For myself wampum is a huge part of my identity as a Wampanoag woman."

The ceremonial uses of wampum were and are multi-fold, woven into belts in mnemonic designs which tell a story to those who know how to read it, whether of history or of creation. They are in many ways the holy books of the people.

Wampum belts kept records. Nosapocket has written that wampum recorded how some of her ancestors, members of the Turtle clan, made trips to Europe during colonization to speak for better treatment. Runners delivered wampum belts used to cement treaties between tribes, nations, clans. They were sent as condolences and invitations, to celebrate events such as births. The way dark and light were woven into a sacred belt could be very complex. Per nativetech.org: "a belt may have white designs on a purple background but be surrounded by a white border, indicating a relationship that was once hostile is now peaceful. A wampum belt painted red was sent as a summons for war."

Perry talks about the emotional alignment and spiritual preparation that goes into making ceremonial things—the community effort.

"Native life was abundant with food, seasons were nice (well, it was cold in winter) so you'd have time to delve into art to perfect your techniques. Now working 9 to 5 jobs we can't just take off for this ceremony or that ceremony" whose complexities take time—as does the creation of objects themselves.

Not only the creation but the passing on of wampum was about having the time, Perry says, "feasting, smoking the sacred pipe, and sharing stories," which surrounded native exchange by barter or reciprocal gift-giving to cement bonds from clan to clan or nation to nation.

This was very different from the use of wampum as the pure cash and carry money of the colonists. "They resented the social niceties of trade. They didn't want to take time to feast and talk; they just wanted their stuff," Perry says.

The thousands of years old practice of creating wampum spread from coastal Algonquians, through trade and giftgiving, west to the Haudenosaunee (Iroquoian confederacy) and on to the Great Lakes, according to Perry. She says that it was not just wampum bartered or gifted. It could be prairie turnips or certain herbs, minerals, metals, anything which was valued.

Then, Isaac de Rasieres, visiting the Dutch colonies in 1627, thought the prestige-carrying beads could work as cash; thus began the use of wampum as money, especially between colonists.

On October 18, 1650, the Massachusetts Bay Colony made wampum official currency. "Strings of eight, 24, 96 and 480 beads were valued, respectively, at one, three and 12 pence and five shillings. Purple beads were worth twice as much as the white ones," Indian Country Today verifies. (Purple was rarer, and more difficult to craft.)

With strings of wampum used as currency, the colonists paid each other, and soon native/colonist interaction also used currency, although native/native use of wampum remained ceremonial. The use of currency corrupted the indigenous lifeway: natives could be paid for furs, valuable to colonial

35. Wampum strings et al at Aptucxet Trading Post (Photo by Lee Roscoe)

36. Wampum jewelry by Carol Lopez and daughter Naomi Walker of White Dove jewelry (Photo by Neil Silberblatt)

37. Wampanoag Day Oct. 12, 2019 at Pilgrim Monument Museum. Darius Coombs teaches hand drilling of wampum (Photo by Lee Roscoe)

business, over-harvest them, forget to hunt at the right times and deplete resources, while colonists reaped the benefits of accumulated wealth.

Perry wishes that "if our modern money was connected to the environment, to reciprocity, social responsibility, it might lead to a more benign society, less destructive use of the environment, healing; instead of toward accumulation, power and greed."

Of course wampum is used for adornment, earrings, bracelets, pendants. (But then even adornments can carry the sacred, can embody the spiritual power of something, symbolize it, and confer its protection or wisdom to the wearer.) Perry's wampum designs may be used by wearers according to their own intention for sacred or secular use, as can her other creations. Creators must be careful while crafting wampum. As with anything created by hand, the spirit not only of the material but of the person who creates the artifact dwells in it; so many tribes believe that one must be in a harmonious if not outright sacred space to create something, lest the bad vibes inhabit it and flow outward.

(It is also important to note that with all meat, fish, shellfish, medicines and plant life harvested, that "following traditional indigenous teachings, nothing goes to waste. When fishing for Quahogs, for instance, the leftover shells are used to make jewelry and the meat is used as food," as Marcus Hendricks, wampum jewelry maker, self-provisioning Mashpee Wampanoag tribal member and cultural educator, points out.)

There are many wonderful wampum artists such as Hendricks of Wampanoag Shells (who also shellfishes as a business, harvesting thus the best of both worlds of the quahog), Jason Widdiss and Hartman Deetz, Carol Lopez and her daughter, Naomi Walker, of the former White Dove jewelry.

Each creator has an individual style, but Perry thinks her creations stand out "because I use nimble hand tools and hand process so I preserve the natural shape of a shell, even if I am carving it to a whale or a bear. You can still see the thickness, weight and presence of the original shell in it."

She creates beads tubular in shape, sometimes round, sometimes circular in flat heishi disks. She will use modern hand drills, but often uses a traditional pump hand drill, essentially a stone wheel, through which a wooden shaft with a stone bit is connected to a wooden handle manipulated by a deerskin or fiber string, a little like a bow. As the assemblage is pumped it bores a hole in shell held by a split piece of wood, or on leather or stone—cooling the process with water. The bead can be smoothed by abrasion of sand and water.

Perry strings her beads with fiber from milkweed, hemp and false nettle which she grows and processes herself. These also go into her twined bags, baskets, belts, tumplines for carrying bags, straps, and twined clothing. She also fashions twined caps, and traditional cedar bark capes and skirts.

Perry also is a creator of bulrush and cattail mats, both woven and twined, and with the former, decorated with natural dye. "I relish hand spinning and using natural dyes which do no harm to people; it's really important; it seeds the soul, which a machine will not do."

38. *Alliance Collar* by Elizabeth James Perry
(Photo by the artist)

Because of her relatives, she had "realistic expectations" for her art. "The culture in our household had a huge input; I cannot conceive of a life without art. Native culture is really creative and healing. It encourages artistry, and I think artistry is really healing—in terms of historical trauma, wanting to stay connected to natural resources in one's homeland. There are a lot of challenges. I struggle with the idea that climate change, pollution and overfishing may limit the resources I need to create with. Hopefully humans will slow the pace of change. It's a lot to reckon with." In the meantime, she wants also to simply revel in her arts and her love for them. And to communicate that joy and love to others.

39. Metacomet (Metacom) in regalia and ceremonial wampum belt, unattributed artist. (Image in public domain)

In 2019, a new ceremonial wampum belt was created and completed.

Project organizer Paula Peters of SmokeSygnals (who created *Our Story*, a series of videos depicting Wampanoag history's significant events to commemorate the Plymouth 400th), says that the new belt was "inspired by the quest for an old one belonging to the Wampanoag sachem, Metacom" also known by the name the British gave him, King Philip. Metacom's nine-inch-wide, nine-foot-long belt signified his status, his bond to the people, and it undoubtedly encompassed spiritual power and tribal history as well.

The original belt was lost to the British, after King Philip's War (1675-6). That war, which was an attempt by the Wampanoag to reclaim its lands from the invading English ended with many natives sent into slavery in the Caribbean, and Metacom's head savagely displayed on a pike in Plymouth.

According to Peters, Benjamin Church (one of the most brutal of English colonial military leaders) proclaimed the belt a spoil of war. It was presented to Massachusetts Governor Josiah Winslow, who passed it to an envoy to deliver to the King of England. It never was received, and its whereabouts to this day are unknown. It was common practice for military victors to steal native wampum, and other artifacts, depriving the original inhabitants of Turtle Island of cultural memory. The 1990 Native American Graves Protection and Repatriation Act ensures for the most part that this can no longer happen, while recognizing the right of tribes to reclaim their heritage. The Wampanoag are hopeful that the original wampum belt will be discovered and repatriated.

Commissioned by the Box Museum in Plymouth, England, the new ceremonial belt toured venues in England from 2020 to 2021 as part of an exhibition about Wampanoag history and culture before returning home to the People.

Linda Coombs, former program director of the Aquinnah Cultural Center and a chair of the Plymouth 400th Wampanoag Advisory Committee, described some of the process, saying that once the purple or white wampum was created it could be woven into the belt. It took longer to make the beads than to weave them into a long strand.

Jason Widdiss, Aquinnah Wampanoag, and Hartman Deetz, Mashpee Wampanoag, created the beads. Julia Marden was the weaving manager. Any Wampanoag could sew on a bead.

At the time of the photos I took, more than 50 tribal members had done so. Fifty more would.

On Wampanoag Day, October 12, 2019, Sharman Brown placed some tubular beads on sinew with a big eye needle, and began to weave them into the warp of the belt being made on the loom. She spoke a feeling likely shared by many of her fellow Wôpanâak, exclaiming, "I can feel this through my whole body!"

TOP LEFT

40. Sharman Brown, Mashpee Wampanoag, working on the ceremonial belt. (Photo by Lee Roscoe)

TOP RIGHT:

41. Wampanoag Day at Pilgrim Monument Museum Provincetown, Paula Peters of SmokeSygnals working on the ceremonial wampum belt (Photo by Lee Roscoe)

LEFT:

42. Steven Peters, Danielle Hill Greendeer, Julia Marden hold the ceremonial belt. (Photo courtesy of Danielle Hill Greendeer)

43. Ceremonial belt created by Wampanoag tribal members (Photo courtesy of SmokeSygnals)

For more on the belt:
https://www.mayflower400uk.org/education/native-america/2020/june/four-hundred-years-of-wampanoag-history/

44. Wampanoag regalia, created by Aquinnah Wampanoag elder Linda Coombs. She and David Weeden in photo
(Photo for Plymouth 400th courtesy of SmokeSygnals)

Regalia

Anita Peters, Mother Bear, is, according to tribal members, the go-to person for making regalia, traditional clothing worn for ceremony, funerals, weddings, and powwows.

She jokes about herself, "I'm the Vera Wang of the tribe."

TOP AND BOTTOM:

45. and 46. Breechclout, leggings, cap and pouch by Mother Bear (Anita Peters)

(Photos courtesy of the artist)

Peters is a revered Mashpee Wampanoag Bear Clan Mother. She says, "In our matriarchal, matrilineal society you get your clan affiliation from your mother's side. The clan mother is chosen by the families, and they in turn chose the male leaders, those who took care of the most people the most—by giving away the most." Mashpee clans include bear, turtle, deer, beaver, otter, eel, eagle and rabbit. Throughout North America's clan systems in general, each animal confers certain attributes and gifts upon the clans which are responsible for certain aspects of governance or tribal life, and in return these clan animals are reciprocated, honored with ceremonial obligations.

To create clothing, the animal, usually deer on the east coast, must be hunted. As in every native culture in America, Anita confirms that "a man would thank the animal for giving its life and kill it in such a way that it did not know what hit it. When animals hold fear, they inject hormones into meat which make it not taste good; fear spoils the meat and changes the spirit of the animal." (As anyone who has eaten poorly killed game knows.)

Traditionally, all parts of the animal are used. Its meat nourishes humans and other animals. Intestines may be used to hold water or encase sausage. Its skin and fur create clothing. Its tendons make sinew for thread. Hooves give glue and rattles and even deer toes (dew claws) can be worn just below the knee to make a rattling sound during dances and ceremony.

47. Painted deerskin skirt by Elizabeth James Perry (Photo by the artist)

48. *Eninuog*, 2017, by Julia Marden approximately 10 inches tall, with deerskin outfits with embroidery floss, hair sash, leg garters, and traditional 17th–18th century trade glass beads
(Photo courtesy of Julia Marden)

49. Mother Bear in clothing inspired by Teeweleema (b. 1836), the last full blood descendant of Ousemequin, the massassoit who interacted with the Plymotheans.
(Photo courtesy of the artist)

50. Mother Bear (Anita Peters) working on regalia near a bit of her miniature Turtle Village
(Photo by Lee Roscoe)

All that remains unused is collected, buried in one place, and thanked with ceremony so that the spirit will return to rejuvenate others of its kind. (This is a complexly nuanced concept; in some native cultures the spirit will urge other animals to feed the people, or it may refurbish itself into a new being and body.) Even as the animal gave life to humans, it is women who, by creating clothing, in a sense also revivify the animal.

Anita grew up in Mashpee in the 1950s, influenced by her great grandmother Mabel Avant (1892-1964) who put on plays and pageants with Wampanoag themes, creating costumes out of cloth so quickly, she amazed Anita with her skill, inspiring her to follow in her grandmother's path.

She attended the Boston School of Fashion Design, learned pattern making, construction and elements of design. "Then I got a job helping clothe 90 Wampanoag men and some women for a National Geographic shoot at Plimoth Plantation" (now Plimoth Patuxet Museums), where she worked for a year in wardrobe and briefly as a cultural interpreter. She's a New England Foundation for the Arts recipient and has made regalia for the Smithsonian and for the exhibit "Captured: 1614," by SmokeSygnals (created as one of a number of videos and panels they designed to show the history and culture of the Wampanoag Nation for the Plymouth 400th).

Mostly Mother Bear delights in creating regalia for her own people, designing traditional men's leggings and breechclouts, moccasins, and women's dresses, consisting of a wrap-around skirt and a one shouldered mantle of four hides sewn together. "The whole outfit can take six deerskins." Anita uses what is left over for pouches, hats, and water bottle carriers.

But she is a modern woman, so she uses commercial deer hides, and waxed linen thread. She cuts her fringes with a spring-loaded scissors and uses modern paints.

In the past hides were brain tanned, sewn with bone needles. "Designs were painted from minerals of graphite, red and yellow ochre, ground up mixed with bear fat applied with little stick. Now I can go to Joanne's Fabrics and there are not many bears there," Anita quips. "Like all cultures, we evolve."

In the late 1800s a woman named Teeweleema (also spelled Terweleema and Tewileema), Metacom's last female descendant, designed unique velvet regalia, highly decorated with laces; about eight women (including Anita) have recently revived those styles.

"I ask people to help me design their regalia, pick colors and designs—so they may help create the symbols painted on the clothing. Many like double curves, triangles and geometrics." She herself favors a design of a whale's tail with waves. One of her own regalia includes the names of nine generations of her family. "When I was at Plimoth we had a catalogue of traditional designs, often men's dreams of hunting which the women interpreted into designs."

51. Breechclout and leggings by Anita Peters
(Photo courtesy of the artist)

Designs and objects of regalia can indicate one's place and status in the clan or tribe, or in a medicine or other society.

A design symbol often essentializes something sacred from a people's shared beliefs and history, clan or tribal affiliation, or from a specific animal, bird, insect or sky worlds, personal journey, other-worldly vision and dream. Symbolic designs confer, in the same way objects created from what is real can, power upon the bearer or wearer, protection; they allow you to carry the spirit of what is symbolized with you, whether worn on one's body as paint, tattoo, as regalia, on a shield, in a medicine pouch, adornment, amulet, or other artifacts.

Many of the artists have mentioned symbolism in their work but cannot elaborate because the spiritual power relating either to tribal belief or personal vision is best kept secret for many reasons, not the least of which is the loss of the spirit power if it is exposed, like water escaping from a container.

Paraphrasing from Barbara Robinson's *Native American Sourcebook*: the real world and the dream or vision world are intertwined in art. A sacred myth, a powerful legend of the tribe or a personal dream or vision might be recorded in pottery, masks, clan symbols, pipe effigy or jewelry, as well as on sand, rock or animal hide. In combining the two worlds, people can increase communication with another spirit or honor the power of that spirit as a protector or benefactor. Thus, the spiritual essence of the animal or plant or element can be represented along with the physical form.

Anita echoes other artists when she says, "I think of positive things when I create the clothing. I think about the people in the circle of ceremony."

As with the *wetu*, the sweat lodge, the ceremonial circle, the circle dance, and the fire circle, the circle is that which encompasses life, and creates equality amongst all within it. Again, so well stated by Robinson: "At the heart of Native beliefs is the circle of nature, which brings connectedness and renewal of resources to the world. Nature's circle can be found in its cycles of the four seasons; its daily cycles; its circle of the compass which includes the four winds or the four directions; and its cycle of life from birth to death to decay to new life."

Mother Bear wears regalia "as much as possible because it is warm in winter, cool and breathable in summer. I wear it with the comfy soft side in, because it feels nice on your skin. The rough side's out, and is easier to paint on."

Regalia may be ornamented with jingling cowrie shells and copper bangles for beauty and for musicality, with bead or quill work, fur and feather trim; there may be shields carried or rattles, headdresses, sashes and garters worn. Regalia for dance events at powwows can be extremely ornate and magnificent, some of it influenced by those of the Plains tribes.

Recently Mother Bear saw a man dressed up in a Halloween costume parody of native dress passing out candy at a public meeting. She was amazed that this kind of disrespect still exists and wondered, "Was he trying to create an incident?"

Dealing with racism is a common exercise, but she says, "You have to keep your sense of humor about it or you can become very angry." An example of her humor: at an event on the Boston Common dedicated to changing the Massachusetts state seal by eliminating the depiction of a sword hanging over a native man's head, Anita reports that "a guy was there with a shield and metal hat and sword. I asked, 'Can I take your picture?' He says. 'Sure,' and I say, 'Because it's really hard to find a racist in the wild like this.'" (Symbols matter, so negative ones such as the state flag and seal's which are perceived to be of colonization and genocidal bloodshed, and which activists native and otherwise have recently successfully sought to have changed, are obviously harmful.) The bumper sticker on Anita's car is "Please Don't Feed the Pilgrims."

"I know racism comes from fear. I know where fear comes from; it means I have the upper hand on you and I just love that."

Under the stars with the air in your lungs, with the sounds of earth, sky, living creatures and water—all of nature is alive and carries spirit power. Nature can offer itself to you to craft objects, whether for material use in providing the needs of living, or of ceremonial use. The hickory, cedar or pine bough or burl which may give you the vision to create flute, bow, or bowl from them, must be asked permission, and once created still carries the sacred essence, the soul, of the nature from which they were fashioned—and must be honored (as with drums, which must be fed with corn meal and tobacco), treated with respect.

Rain, Wind, Stone, Stars, Forest, Earth, Water, Four Leggeds, Wingeds, not all those can be converted into objects but those that are will themselves be sacred and their physical and spiritual attributes remain essentialized, conferring that power on the humans, especially in what is worn: whether in such as fox fur carrying the intelligence of that animal, copper carrying attributes of fire and blood, or feathers carrying the vision of the hawk, the swift silence of the owl, or the gifts of the Creator through the messenger of eagle.

52. *Veteran's Star Medallion* by Jonathan Perry
(Photo courtesy of the Institute of American Indian Arts)

Adornment

While influenced by his ancestors' carvings and jewelry, and using their means, methods and materials, Jonathan Perry's art makes a stunning transition from the traditional to the new, creating objects which are unique and original.

"I am inspired by the past, defined by the environment, and by myself, my current reality. By water, weather; belief systems, stories, and what reveals itself to me in the material itself, the hues, the grains. I listen to the material."

Jonathan James Perry, like his sister Elizabeth, was surrounded by his culture and its artisans growing up. There were classically trained musicians amongst his relatives, too.

Living now in North Providence, he is still very connected to his Aquinnah Wampanoag people, serving on the tribal council and involved in historical preservation and ceremonial participation. He is the quintessential whole indigenous man, competent in the arts of living, creating and providing, but also very much adapted to the modern world.

53. Heron Collar by Jonathan Perry featured in Native Fashion Now, at Peabody Essex Museum (Photo courtesy of Peabody Essex Museum)

He practices subsistence by hunting, fishing, gathering, and processing foods. He builds traditional houses, performs by drumming, singing and dancing in groups like the Iron River Singers and the Wampanoag Nation Singers and Dancers (which the late, revered Alice Lopez, and Tony Pollard, Nanepashemet, as well as Darrel Wixon and Nosapocket, founded). He's won numerous grants and awards including a First People's Fund Community Spirit Award. He's been an advisor to, and an exhibitor and performer at, numerous museums, including the Museum of the American Indian, the Harvard Peabody Museum, the Peabody Essex Museum, Maine's Abbe Museum and the New Bedford Whaling Museum. He was with Plimoth Patuxet Museums for 13 years, and was the native program manager for many of those years.

Learning native metallurgy and carving from fellow practitioners from his teenage years on, he is now a consummate carver and jewelry creator.

His copper pieces are cold hammered; that is a process by which metal is annealed using heat and quick cooling to make it malleable for expansion, drawing it out into a sheet form to shape it. (The copper is not melted and poured into a mold.) Results, such as his *Harpoon Earrings*, pulse with a mystical spirit and classic modernity.

He crafts tools of stone but says, "I also use drills and metal drill bits as I am a modern native artist and can incorporate any technology." As his ancestors did, he handrocks

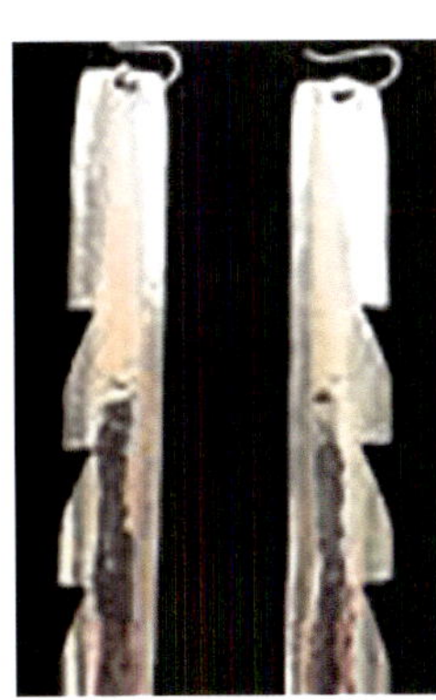

54. *Harpoon Earrings*, left, and 55. *Balanced Face* right, by Jonathan Perry (Photos courtesy of the artist's website)

56. *Pukwudgie Pipe* by Jonathan Perry (Photo courtesy of Mashantucket Pequot Museum and Research Center)

designs into the piece by pounding and pressing or rocking a curved blade to press an incised design to the soft metal, freehand, and by eye. It's physically hard and time consuming because no machinery is used. He can only "rock" for about fifteen minutes at a time.

In the past, copper was traded along indigenous routes, especially from the Great Lakes region. It was also gathered from lake bogs in Wampanoag turf, as well as from a Rhode Island quarry said to be the finest on earth until colonists played it out—around the same time that they outlawed native wearing of copper and other ornamentations.

The Wampanoag were considerate in their harvesting of metal. Perry comments that there was more of it around then than today as he reiterates what other of the artists have stressed, that Wampanoag people were as care-giving in their harvest of metals as they were in hunting and gathering, taking only part of a plant so it would grow back stronger, leaving enough animals to reproduce and to feed their own. Never taking all.

Carving from wood, whether small or large objects, such as bowls and dugout canoes shaped with fire and hand tools, is very different, Perry says, from carving in ivory, bone or stone or shell.

Using hand-made tools he himself crafted, he has fashioned pipes using softer minerals such as catlinite, traded for from Minnesota, or locally sourced steatite (talc, soapstone) from the Blue Hills of Massachusetts or Rhode Island. (One of his pipes was featured on the 2011 Sacagawea coin which commemorated the 1621 peace treaty between Plymouth colony and the Wampanoag.)

To finish the stem, "I use a hardwood shaft and a pinch of sand on some of my pipes. You cut an x into the hardwood shaft, then you put a pinch of sand and start twisting the shaft." Abrasives such as sandstones and smoked sharkskin polish the finalized piece.

Igneous rocks are harder and must be arduously pecked. Water is not usually part of the process, he says, unless you are working on shell. Then besides keeping the dust down it cools the shell during the tooling.

Perry's pieces reflect Wampanoag philosophy and belief. For example, Balanced Face is a "hand-carved face effigy on ivory with scrimshaw serpent, thunderbird, and traditional tattoo designs."

I ask whether the juxtaposed horned serpent with thunderbirds is related to the Anishinaabe's belief in which the thunder beings balance with the underwater serpents. (For Great Lakes people, the underwater beings indicated where copper was and protected it.) "All Algonquian belief is similar," Perry says. "It is balance, the duality of the above world and the below world. It's like why you braid your hair; you are bringing together mind, body and spirit, every day. If not, you go out of balance and become unhealthy."

FACING PAGE:
57. Robert Peters holding his work
***The Honor Beat,* 54"w x 44"h acrylic on canvas**
(Photo by Mario Soares)

Painting

58. *Exile* by Robert Peters, 8'w x 4'h, acrylic on canvas (Courtesy of the artist)

Painting As Healing

Traditional objects and vision infuse the work of the indigenous artists who practice an art attenuated from functionality, per se. Native art for art's sake is a result of the Settler culture's influence, yet it almost always maintains elements of sacred symbolism and of nature's influence within it.

Robert Peters represents that modern fusion.

Peters does not do traditional Wampanoag arts; rather, he uses indigenous influences from many tribes including his own throughout his small but intense body of paintings and drawings. A good selection of his art, poetry and musings appears in a calendar produced for 2020, entitled *Thirteen Moons, a Meditation on Indigenous Life.*

He writes in the calendar, "I was driven from the lodge to be shown that we cannot go back to the ancient ways, but we must keep them, we must use them, expand upon the knowledge the ancient ones have passed down through generations. Use the knowledge given to you in your dreams. Look for the things the Creator is trying to show us."

He tells me, "I want to depict the way we are now," not the past, although the past informs the present through the continuation of traditions, particularly ceremonial ones. "We're here right now, this is what we experience now, this is what we go through now. That's what I know."

Peters is from a distinguished Wampanoag family. His cousins are Ramona Peters (Nosapocket), Anita Peters (Mother Bear), and traditionalist Jim Peters. His father was author and activist Russell Peters (Fast Turtle). Paula Peters who runs SmokeSygnals and is also a well-known journalist, is his sister. The late, and very much missed medicine man, John Peters (Slow Turtle), was his uncle.

He's a retired MBTA employee, a "motor person" (train operator), who was born in Philadelphia, lived in Germantown there, a mixed urban area, moved to Natick (into what he calls a middle class white suburban neighborhood) and then to Mashpee. Now he lives in Boston, staying close to southern Massachusetts. His signature is a curlicue representing the Mashpee River and himself, meaning "I don't go very far." His blue-collar gestalt is as much a part of his work as his native heritage.

Peters didn't train as an artist, though he did take drawing classes in college and learned the technology of Photoshop and Dreamweaver. But his technique is "self-developed." He paints with acrylic but says he did a "self-exercise for three years when I did not draw with a pencil but only in pen." He thinks some of his best work derived from that. In 2007 when he retired, he started doing more art though he had been painting since the early 90s.

His work is known and beloved by his fellow tribespeople and adorns many of their homes and workplaces. He's exhibited at the Mashantucket Pequot Museum and Cotuit Center for the Arts. He'd like to see his 25 major pieces exhibited altogether in a museum or gallery. He sells on his website and brings calendars and prints to powwows. He cautions that his motive is not money; he paints because something moves him to create.

59. *The First Round* by Robert Peters, 30"w x 40"h, acrylic on canvas (Courtesy of the artist)

60. *Contemplating the Universe* by Robert Peters, 24"w x 48"h acrylic on canvas (Courtesy of the artist)

This interview has been edited and in some cases paraphrases are used for clarity.

LR: You seem to live between many worlds, spirit/dream, the visionary and the so-called real world, between work and art, between your heritages as black, red and white racially. Are you constantly balancing those many worlds?

RP: Any native person struggles with the duality between their culture and being a part of the American culture, so you have to walk that line. We might believe things one way, but then we go to work and do something for a living that totally goes against our beliefs. So that's something people struggle with. They also live with the past, the loss of the past; so I think where that's true for me it's true for most native people and it doesn't mean I don't have both feet on the ground or am not totally engaged in the conversation—it's just that there are other things that we consider.

LR: And that split seems to reveal itself in your art.

RP: One of the first pieces I created was a drawing of a lone wolf howling in the middle of a city on a bluff. There's no name for it. I just say it's me.

(In *Exile*, his largest work, a 4 by 8-foot canvas, the same bewildering city slants in its beautiful ugliness like a drunken forest. "I was a spiritual exile. The trees sent me away. They instructed me to live in the white man's world and not return until I achieved the kind of success that white men aspired to have," his verse accompanying the painting explains.)

RP: The loss of the past keeps us in the spirit world.

LR: Because of that loss you dwell in the spirit world or...?

RP: Well, I mean our historic loss, that we are a people who experienced genocide and then the modern losses: suicide, addiction. We lose so many people from addiction we go to funerals every month. So, there's the immediate loss that keeps us going back to the old Indian cemetery. We're there too much.

LR: The spirit world is solace? Escape?

RP: (No answer).

LR: Your art seems to live in the spirit world. In the calendar you speak of visions in a blue light: spirits from the Great Swamp in Rhode Island where Pometacomet (King Philip) suffered defeat, and of ancestors singing in the wind when you were the sole keeper of the medicine fire.

RP: I think the only time I really was part of spirit world was with an experience

61. Robert Peters untitled wolf drawing, the one he says is himself
(Courtesy of the artist)

62. ***Rage Against the Machine*** **by Robert Peters, 36"w x 36"h, acrylic on canvas** (Courtesy of the artist)

with blue light that lasted about a month. I was exhausted but awakened—and I had a foot in both worlds.

I'm asking myself, is this really happening? Did I really have these experiences here and there, because there were a lot more than the ones I am telling about—then I found something I had written, years earlier: "with the conclusion of every successive episode in time comes a new reality." That was my answer and it came from myself in the past. When you pay attention to things ... I think everybody has this connection but they don't pay attention or they doubt it ... when you pay attention it's telling you things you might not be ready to accept, you may not have the capacity to absorb it, but you're being given answers.

LR: There's a through-line theme about coming home I really identify with. I once tried to create a ritual of the loss of connection to the natural world and the return to it.

RP: I appreciate that you identify with the theme of home. I appreciate that, because that is really a central point, that connects everybody, everybody has that concept of home, that they want to hold onto.

One of the things I stress is that we give up so much of our power, by throwing our voices out there into infinity as when we go online. Anyone can use our voices if they want to; and giving up our voice is an important part of what we give up. By coming back to the fire with each other and returning to our traditions and its circle we can bring our voices back, bring power back.

(He writes in his Calendar book about not being at home living in someone else's world, "and that world pushes the environment away.")

LR: You see the animals coming home too, right?

RP: I love the fact that people, the creatures and the environment are all talked about in the same conversation in this calendar.

LR: In a painting of a sweat lodge, animal spirits are entering the lodge with the human beings.

RP: Well, they really did. I painted and painted and as I did, the duck's head came down and then I saw the cat, and then kept seeing these other animals which kept coming in and then there was a guy lifting another guy; they just all came in on their own.

LR: Fiction writers talk about characters entering on their own. Does that happen often when you are painting?

RP: If it does, I let it.

LR: Being around the medicine fire is a predominant theme in your work (I realize fire can be the center of home)—tell me a bit about that fire, how it reveals itself in your art, what it means.

RP: Bringing these performances back to a circle around the fire, and having the tradition of being around a fire and being together addressing our ideas, is a very important way to take back power, it's a natural thing which we do. The medicine fire, the artwork and the poetry are all connected, they're all connected tissues in that the things that happened that made me create the artwork and the poetry are also the same things that made us light the medicine fire in 2001.

(Peters tells me that before 9/11 happened, he felt an urge to start a new medicine fire for his people to somehow make right the weird vibes in his world at the time. The fire lasted for ten years, every Thanksgiving weekend. Peters explains that a firekeeper is a person who takes responsibility for the fire and keeps it; burning fires for those who have passed, keeping protocol, smudging entrants, making sure no alcohol enters the circle, and that males and females enter in a traditional way.)

RP: At one fire, there was a fifty mile an hour wind and driving rain and I tell that story in the calendar book. I didn't really understand how important it was when I wrote it, or exactly everything that it meant. And I get new meanings from it all the time. I discover little things and say oh OK.

LR: Do you mean you didn't know all of what it meant when you wrote the book or created the fires?

RP: All of the above. When you start writing something, or painting something, you may not exactly know why you are writing it. With the Honor Beat (a painting which took years to finish, depicting six men singing and drumming), there were three inspirations (including the medicine, the wind and blue light). The first was when I sat at the drum. When I missed the beat, they charged me a dollar. As time goes by and things happen to us in the time between . . . things become even more real than when I wrote it.

LR: This happens with your paintings, too?

RP: There's a painting with everybody around the fire and a woman ended up standing in the background I did not recall consciously who had been there. It slipped my mind but it didn't slip my paintbrush.

LR: Tell me about the African man wearing ammunition on his head, *Contemplating the Universe*.

RP: It's based on an unexplained photo in National Geographic. I just kept going back to it and really was intrigued by it; you don't know if the guy is bad or good, but you do wonder what he is thinking. You contemplate the universe and the universe contemplates you, especially (he laughs) when you are wearing your bullets on your head. . . .

My calendar is about understanding and healing. The art of storytelling can be revived in our culture and be powerful healing it.

(In addition to his own art, he is part of a healing project with the state's Bureau of Substance Abuse Services. He created a book as a kind of stomp dance. The idea was stomp out the culture of addiction with native kids. He's working on new curriculum with the University of Massachusetts and the bureau.)

RP: One lesson is to take a piece of wood that will comprise a box kids keep their pencils or ceremonial items in. We use a piece of wood and stain paint onto the grain; we paint what the wood is saying, then they paint themselves, their own view of their self. The image represents what you believe.

63. ***One Sustains Us, One Does Not*** **by Emma Jo Mills Brennan, fabric art with beads and embroidery commissioned 1996 for Mashpee Wampanoag Museum** (Photo of giclee by Ned Manter)

Mixed Media

64. Emma Jo Mills Brennan with her weaving, *Eastern Peoples* (Photo by Lee Roscoe)

Tribal influence of symbolism and reverence for nature emerge in modern interpretations in the work of Ej (Emma Jo) Mills Brennan.

Ej is, like so many of her Wampanoag peers, a multi-verse, a multi-media artist. I visited her in the cranberry red house on protected land which has been sacred to her people for thousands of years (and land dear to me, for I was part of a group that helped save 300 acres of it from development as a golf course).

The house, with its pine panel walls and 1950s stone-like vinyl floors, is surrounded by pitch pine and black oak trees through which Santuit Pond changes light moodily. Situated at the end of a long dirt road, Ej's beloved Shetland sheep, two coal, two cream and beige coated, are eating grass and hay within an enclosure. It's a beautiful, peaceful, inspiring—even sacred setting. One would almost have to do art, living there.

Ej's mother was the daughter of Italian immigrants. Her father was Mashpee Wampanoag. Her parents met and married on the isle of Capri in Italy while he was serving in World War II, returning after the war to reside in Mashpee. "I have the best of both worlds," Ej says.

Both parents were hardworking and creative. Ej's mother wrote, drew and made

65. *Corn Meal* by Emma Jo Mills Brennan, *giclee of watercolor*
(Photo by Lee Roscoe)

ceramic flowers so delicate they looked real. Her father, Elwood Mills Sr., Lone Goose, who owned the Ockry Trading Post, a Mashpee landmark for years, hand built the family house in which Ej lives.

Ej says her father was "a true hunter, fisherman and guide (as were his father and uncles before him). He provided for his family off the land: one deer a year, geese, quail, partridge, ducks, fish, shellfish and more." The Millses were part of an extended family which gathered and prepared sustenance communally.

That deep connection to the tribe infuses much of her art. Paintings of pots, baskets and drums, on beaches and shorelines at sunrise or sunset, are very much a signifier of her voice. They are artifacts of her people and they are offerings, she explains, both in themselves and in what she depicts them carrying. "One pot contains cornmeal, and near another there are quahogs which are sustenance, as food, biologically and also spiritually."

She shows me *Breast Plate in the Sky*, a gouache painting. Streaks of clouds across a blurry moon, in monochromes of greys, charcoals and white, with a subtle touch of green, within a massive gold frame. "This was the view one night traveling on Route 6, and it brought to mind one of our Tribal Dancers who passed too soon. Returning home, I was compelled to paint through the night, completing it in one sitting."

She has also designed wampum jewelry and beadwork and has illustrated student books, including one of prayers for the Wôpanâak Language Reclamation Project's school. (She can speak the language a little bit, telling me in English that her native name is Little Rain Drop.)

Eastern People, a weaving which took a few years off and on, has a southwestern feel but its symbolism is Ej's own vision: "The fringe represents Roots to the Elements/Darkness encases Light of the Spirit. That Spirit within Each of Us /As the Sun Rises, Birth of Spirit breaks darkness and Travels its Arrow Journey to Creator," she writes.

"I do art, for the exploration and reflection it allows me to experience. It's of the beauty of the earth and the natural world. All of my work is related to my love of life and for the earth, even when abstract. It's a spiritual realm, a meditation."

Bringing out a painting of ospreys based on a photo she took at a nearby estuary, Ej comments, "I prefer to work from photos, as I couldn't do justice for the big birds otherwise. Do I need more grasses? Do I need bark?" (Answering herself): "It's a dead tree, so there is no bark.

"I love the look of things that are almost done," she continues. "This is what happens with some of my work; I just let it be." Another painting of Canada Geese eating grass pleases her, though their locale is pedestrian: at the local dump. "It's so simple and beautiful somehow just the way it is; I don't want to add anything more. It's fulfilling as it is; they are so beautiful.

66. *The Gatherer*, by Emma Jo Mills Brennan, fabric, felt, applique, embroidery 1988 (Photo by Ned Manter)

67. Wet felt crafted by Emma Jo Mills Brennan, (Photo courtesy of the artist)

68. *Breast-Plate in the Sky* by Emma Jo Mills Brennan
Gouache, 2008 or later (Photo courtesy of artist)

"I'm very color conscious. I love the night sky, the changes throughout the time of day. I enjoy observing and taking it all in. Especially all the little nuances that animals display. To try to transmit it out is the big challenge."

One of her pieces, *One Sustains Us, One Does Not,* is permanently exhibited at the Mashpee Wampanoag Museum. "This was a larger commissioned work and required an environmental theme. So, I chose to show all the wildlife that was covered, by creating a golf course. The now disappeared pollywogs' eggs, pollywogs, snakes, turtles, frogs and fish were designed, beaded and embroidered, from the bottom up, as in a bog ditch." Embroidered across the top of the work is a linear pattern of golf tees, each with a golf ball, hole marker, flag and dollar sign. "A lot of people have said the piece really hits home. We used to walk the bog ditches and explore as kids, and we knew that it provided sustenance too. The ditch would be black with pollywogs, wagging their little tails. Now did anyone inform all the LIFE in those ditches, before they just filled it in with gravel?

"This world . . . we just cover life like that. We come from the earth and we should live off the earth. Today it's all exploited. We are all so consumed by modern culture, our computer screens, our passwords, it's not healthy, it's causing stress. How many people don't do an art form because they're tapping keys and consumed with computerized socialization? There's a real lack of true vision, seeing true colors, looking at Creator's gifts, the true essence of creation. Today we can see the burden of earth's destruction, the buildings . . . for miles, destroying the natural growth patterns, the fields, the water sources. We don't need all this ridiculousness, it's epic. What are we doing?"

This sentiment is echoed in one of Ej's original compositions from her CD series,

"Breath of Prayer III: Have You Seen the Moon Tonight?" "Can we take the time, to realign, our thoughts, our ways, Oh can we, Will we?" On "Breath of Prayers II" Ej plays solo songs for cedar flute she composed, paying homage to the tribe (and to the instrument itself) using a gifted flute, handmade by Ramona Peters of white cedar (a sacred Wampanoag plant-world offering, along with others such as red cedar, sweetgrass and tobacco).

Ej is connected to the land through her sheep, too. ("I love them. They are so peaceful.") And though she's scraped out manure every morning for ten years, she says they are much easier to care for than dogs. "I love working with wool and wearing wool" because wool is not artificial, but natural. Someone else shears the sheep, but those shearings led her to try wet-felting. "The fibers swim in the hot soapy water; then in cold water they lock together. It's labor intensive, with a lot of kneading and rolling, but eventually you get results" which have a life of their own. "I created a piece which looked like it had a tree in it; the tree looked real because of the fibers, and the natural colors of the sheep."

The textural quality of felting leads her to comment that at heart she is a sculptor. She has created numerous sensuous abstract "Henry Moore-ish" clay nudes, and masks of distinctly Wampanoag faces, and she tries to give her two-dimensional art a three-dimensionality whether it is creating fabric art, paintings, or block prints.

Ej trained in visual arts and music, but also taught herself wood block printing, felting and weaving, the latter by using a wall-hung frame, big sewing needles, her fingers and a hair pin. "I don't like a loom with a shuttle. I just experimented."

She's exhibited at the Boston Children's Museum, the Mashantucket Pequot Museum, and many a powwow, Unitarian Universalist church, and art fair. She's a New England Foundation for the Arts recipient.

As proprietor of HAN DUN—Studio, Gallery & Shop in the Mashpee/Falmouth area for many years, Ej was always very inspired to feature other artists' works. Hers can be seen at Wampanoag Trading Post & Gallery in Mashpee, started by Mashpee Wampanoag Paula Peters and Danielle Hill Greendeer. She says it's exciting that more Wampanoag artists are becoming more visible, as has the culture, and this is really good for the people. She speaks for many of her people when she suggests that all cultures return to their roots, reviving a more natural way of living, and not "cover life over" with mindless development.

In Conclusion

In our modern society we lack the primary skills to create provisioning, self-sufficiently. Most of us live in a secondary sufficiency, purchasing and consuming that which is made for us. We do not supply ourselves from nature with the basic needs of food, shelter, clothing and energy for heat, light and cooking. Nor do we usually create our own first-hand, in place, music, dance, and story.

It is important to stress that in Wampanoag life, many of the artifacts of self-provisioning for material needs, as well as providing for music, dance, story and other needs of the heart, are critically important—all would take another book to do justice. There are for example, tools to scrape and prepare hides and clothing; bows, arrows and snares for hunting; nets and weirs for fishing; *mishoons* for water travel; creations containing curative and sacred medicine; drums, flutes and other musical devices; and the tools and methods of planting and harvesting. There are still many amongst the Wampanoag and other indigenous people practicing skills highly honed through generations who combine material and sacred traditions in both the crafting and the usage of those "makings."

Indeed, the list of vibrant Wampanoag artists and artisans is long, and I have by no means covered them all. There are writers such as Earl Mills, Woody Mills and the late Amelia Bingham; musicians and playwrights like M'walim ("DaPhunkee Professor") and numerous drumming, singing and dancing groups. There are multi-talented twiners, potters and regalia makers such as Kerri Helme, Marlene Lopez, and Aquinnah Wampanoag Rabbit Clan mother Linda Coombs, and *mishoon* and arrow makers such as Philip Wynne Many Hands, artisans such as Darrel Wixon, painters like Ryan Darby. There are founding elders, artisans such as the late Gladys Widdiss, who popularized multi-colored pottery from the Gay Head Cliffs of Aquinnah, and many Vanderhoops of the same area, practicing pottery and wampum jewelry both in the past and the present. There are videographers and writers such as respected journalist and founder of SmokeSygnals Paula Peters and her son Steven. There are esteemed history keepers such as the late Betty Hendricks, teachers such as the late Nancy Eldredge (Wuskowon), and Gertrude "Kitty" Hendricks, jessie little doe Baird, founder of the Wôpanâak Language Reclamation Project, and so many others who contribute so much to tribal culture.

And, of course, there are those artists yet unborn who will carry on the future seven generations, ever evolving, ever conserving the vital culture and arts of those who are our hosts upon this land.

For as Elizabeth James Perry notes, "There are times when culture goes underground due to intolerance; however, you can't kill a spirit and you can't kill spiritual beliefs. The connections are real, and our Wampanoag beliefs and arts continue in the present."

69. Fall Village (Photo courtesy Institute for American Indian Studies)

70. Aquinnah Wampanoag potters made vases, bowls, and other souvenirs from the colorful Gay Head cliffs. Gladys Widdis made the bowl in the center of this photo in 1994. The vases on the left and right were made by unknown potters in the late 19th and early 20th centuries.
(Photo by Wayne Smith, courtesy of the Martha's Vineyard Museum)

Appendix

To view Wampanoag arts and culture as of this writing, see below. Some of these sites also include representation of art from other indigenous nations. Note that Mashpee and Aquinnah are centers for the federally recognized tribes of the Mashpee Wampanoag and the Aquinnah Wampanoag, and that Plymouth is a nexus for the historic meeting of Colonists with Wampanoag.

With all these venues it is a good idea to check ahead to find out what is currently on exhibit.

Cape Cod and The Islands

BOURNE

Aptucxet Trading Post Museum
6 Aptucxet Rd, Bourne, MA 02532
508-759-8167
https://www.bournehistoricalsociety.org/aptucxet-museum/

BREWSTER

Cape Cod Museum of Natural History
869 Main St Route 6A, Brewster, MA 02631
508-896-3867
https://www.ccmnh.org/

Brewster Historical Society
739 Lower Rd, Brewster, PO Box 1146, MA 02631
508-896-9521
https://www.brewsterhistoricalsociety.org/

CHATHAM

Atwood House Museum
347 Stage Harbor Rd, Chatham, MA 02633
508-945-2493
https://chathamhistoricalsociety.org/
(Has a *wetu* built by David Weeden THPO, Tribal Historic Preservation Officer and tribal councilman for the Mashpee Wampanoag, with his son.)

COTUIT

Cahoon Museum of American Art
4676 Falmouth Rd, P.O. Box 1853, Cotuit, MA_02635
508-428-7581
https://cahoonmuseum.org/

DENNIS

Cape Cod Museum of Art
60 Hope Ln, Dennis, MA 02638
508-385-4477
https://www.ccmoa.org/

EASTHAM

Cape Cod National Seashore Salt Pond Visitor Center
50 Nauset Rd, Eastham, MA 02642
508-255-3421
https://www.nps.gov/caco/index.htm

Eastham Historical Society
1741 Swift-Daley House
2375 Route 6, PO Box 8, Eastham, MA 02642
508-240-1247

1869 Schoolhouse Museum
25 Schoolhouse Road, Eastham, MA 02642
508-255-0788
easthamhistorical@verizon.net

Eastham Public Library
190 Samoset Road, Eastham, MA 02642
508-240-5950
https://easthamlibrary.org/
(Robert Peters painting in entryway.)
Also www.easthamlibrary.org Eastham 400th videos; see "Native American" playlist.)

HARWICH

Harwich Conservation Trust
947 MA-28, Harwich, MA 02645
508-432-3997
harwichconservationtrust.org
(Native Lands walks with Marcus Hendricks and Todd Kelley.)

MARTHAS VINEYARD

Aquinnah Wampanoag Tribe of Gay Head
Aquinnah Cultural Center
Aquinnah Wampanoag Indian Museum
35 Aquinnah Circle, Aquinnah, MA 02535
508-645-7900
https://www.aquinnah.org/

Martha's Vineyard Museum
151 Lagoon Pond Rd, Vineyard Haven, MA 02568
508-627-4441
https://mvmuseum.org/

MASHPEE

Mashpee Archives
13 Great Neck Rd N, Mashpee, MA 02649
508-539-1438
https://www.mashpeema.gov/historical-commission/events/197511

Mashpee Public Library
64 Steeple St, Mashpee, MA 02649
508-539-1435
https://mashpeepubliclibrary.org/

Mashpee Wampanoag Tribal Council
483 Great Neck Rd S, Mashpee, MA 02649
508-477-0208
https://mashpeewampanoagtribe-nsn.gov/
(The Mashpee Powwow takes place over July 4th weekend at Mashpee Wampanoag Tribal Council HQ.)

Old Indian Meeting House
410 Meetinghouse Road, Mashpee, MA 02649
508-477-0208
https://mashpeewampanoagtribe-nsn.gov/old-indian-meeting-house
(The oldest Native American church on the east coast of the U.S.)

Wampanoag Tribal Museum
414 Main St, Mashpee, MA 02649
508-477-9339
https://mashpeewampanoagtribe-nsn.gov/museum

Wampanoag Trading Post and Gallery
20 North Street, Mashpee, MA 02649
774-361-6704
https://www.wampanoagtradingpostandgallery.com/
(Tribal members maintain a year-round retail store for Native American art, also online.)

The Native Land Conservancy
http://www.nativelandconservancy.org/about-nlc.html

Wôpanâak Language Reclamation Project
https://wlrp.org

NANTUCKET

Nantucket Whaling Museum and Historical Association
15 Broad St, Nantucket, MA 02554
508-228-1894
https://nha.org/

ORLEANS

Orleans Historical Society
3 River Rd, Orleans, MA 02653
508-240-1329
https://www.orleanshistoricalsociety.org/

PROVINCETOWN

Pilgrim Monument and Provincetown Museum
1 High Pole Hill Rd, Provincetown, MA 02657
508-487-1310
https://www.pilgrim-monument.org/
(Features "Our Story: The Complicated Relationship of the Indigenous Wampanoag and the Mayflower Pilgrims." In partnership with SmokeSygnals.)

TRURO

The Highland House Museum and Truro Historical Society
6 Highland Light Rd, Truro, MA 02666
508-487-3397
https://trurohistoricalsociety.org/highlandhouse/
(Featuring "Wampanoag Nation: People of the First Light." As of this writing, displaying Julia Marden's 4 wampum belt history: "The Ancient Ones, The Home Site, Plague, War, Slavery, Powwow Time.")

WELLFLEET

Wellfleet Historical Society Museum
266 Main St, Wellfleet, MA 02667
508-349-9157
http://www.wellfleethistoricalsociety.org/

YARMOUTH

Taylor-Bray Farm
108 Bray Farm Rd N, Yarmouth Port, MA 02675
774-251-1869
https://www.taylorbrayfarm.org/
(Artifacts, archeological digs.)

The Historical Society of Old Yarmouth,
229 Old King's Highway (Route 6A), P.O. Box 11, Yarmouth Port, MA 02675
508-362.3021
https://www.hsoy.org/
(In the Spring of 2020, Marcus Hendricks began working on the Turtle *Wetu* Project in collaboration with the Yarmouth Historical Society. This is an ongoing project that will include a series of walks discussing indigenous history from the local area, as well as festivals celebrating local indigenous culture. You can find more information on this through the Old Yarmouth Historical Society website: http://hsoy.org/coming-events-1.)

Other places in Massachusetts

BOSTON

The Museum of Fine Arts
465 Huntington Ave, Boston, MA 02115
617-267-9300
https://www.mfa.org/
(Indigenous People's Day, usually in October: https://www.mfa.org/event/community-celebrations/indigenous-peoples-day?event=3172.)

Boston Children's Museum
308 Congress St, Boston, MA 02210
617-426-6500
bostonchildrensmuseum.org

Massachusetts Historical Society
1154 Boylston St, Boston, MA 02215
617-536-1608
http://www.masshist.org/

New England Foundation for the Arts
1000 Washington Street, Second Floor, Boston, MA 02118T
617-951-0010
https://www.nefa.org/

CAMBRIDGE

Harvard University Peabody Museum
11 Divinity Ave, Cambridge, MA 02138
617-496-1027
https://www.peabody.harvard.edu/
https://www.peabody.harvard.edu/listening-to-wampano-ag-voices-beyond-1620

MIDDLEBOROUGH

Robbins Museum of Archeology
17 Jackson St, Middleborough, MA 02346
508-947-9005
https://www.massarchaeology.org/robbins-museum/about-the-museum/

NEW BEDFORD

New Bedford Whaling Museum
18 Johnny Cake Hill, New Bedford, MA 02740
508-997-0046
https://www.whalingmuseum.org/

PLYMOUTH

Herring Pond Wampanoag Meeting House
128 Herring Pond Road, Plymouth, MA 02360
https://www.herringpondtribe.org/page/5/

PILGRIM HALL

75 Court St. Plymouth, MA 02360
508-746-1620
https://pilgrimhall.org/

Plymouth 400th, https://www.plymouth400inc.org/

Plimoth Patuxet Museums
(formerly Plimoth Plantation)
137 Warren Ave, Plymouth, MA 02360
508-746-1622
https://plimoth.org/
(Known for its Wampanoag program and village, as well as its Pilgrim village and enactments.)

SALEM

Peabody Essex Museum
161 Essex St, Salem, MA 01970
978-745-9500
https://www.pem.org/

Other New England Venues

CONNECTICUT

Mashantucket Pequot Museum and Research Center
110 Pequot Trail, Ledyard, CT 06338
800-411-9671, 860-396-6910
https://www.pequotmuseum.org/

Yale University Art Gallery
1111 Chapel St, New Haven, CT 06510
203-432-0600
https://artgallery.yale.edu/

Institute for American Indian Studies
38 Curtis Rd, Washington, CT 06793
860-868-0518
https://www.iaismuseum.org/

MAINE

Abbe Museum
26 Mt Desert St, Bar Harbor, ME 04609
207-288-3519
https://www.abbemuseum.org/
(Wabanaki Nations information and exhibits)

NEW HAMPSHIRE

Hood Museum of Art, Dartmouth
6 East Wheelock St. Hanover, N.H. 03755
603-646-2808
https://hoodmuseum.dartmouth.edu/

Mt. Kearsage Indian Museum
18 Highlawn Rd, Warner, NH 03278
603-456-2600
https://www.indianmuseum.org/

RHODE ISLAND

Tomaquag Museum
390A Summit Rd, Exeter, RI 02822
401-491-9063
https://www.tomaquagmuseum.org/

Other Parts of the USA

MINNESOTA

Minnesota Museum of American Art
350 Robert St N, St Paul, MN 55101
651-797-2571
https://mmaa.org/

NEW YORK

Metropolitan Museum of Art
1000 5th Ave, New York, NY 10028
212-535-7710
https://www.metmuseum.org/

National Museum of the American Indian
Alexander Hamilton U.S. Custom House One Bowling Green, New York, NY 10004
212-514-3700
https://americanindian.si.edu/visit/reopening-ny

WASHINGTON, D.C.

The Smithsonian's National Museum of the American Indian
4th St. and Independence Ave. SW, Washington, DC 20560
202-633-1000
https://americanindian.si.edu/

WISCONSIN

Wisconsin Museum of Quilts and Fiber Arts
N50 W5050, Portland Rd, Cedarburg, WI 53012
262-546-0300
https://www.wiquiltmuseum.com

The UK

The Box Museum
Tavistock Pl, Plymouth PL4 8AX, United Kingdom
+44-1752-304774
https://www.theboxplymouth.com/
(The Box exhibited Wampanoag artifacts for the 400th, including the Mashpee Wampanoag ceremonial wampum belt, as well as giving the Wampanoag ongoing voice in videos and other exhibits, including pottery and archaeological artifacts. Online at: Mayflower 400: Old Worcestershire & New Plymouth (Part II) - Worcestershire Archive & Archaeology Service (explorethepast.co.uk.)

Video

For "Our Story" Four Hundred Years of Wampanoag History created by SmokeSygnals
http://www.plymouth400inc.org/OurStory
https://www.youtube.com/playlist?list=PL_SEJpPfEF9wgV3few2-8rwKHHXmFJ8uu

ARTISTS' SITES

Many of the sites in the Appendix have special events, gift stores, and native artisans' markets. The individual artists mentioned in the brochure have Facebook and Etsy sites. They would appreciate your patronage. Some are listed below.

Hartman Deetz
https://ockwaybaywampum.com

Kerri Ann Helme
https://www.facebook.com/Dawnlanddesigns

Marcus Hendricks
https://wampanoagshells.com/

Julia Marden Bluejay's Vision
https://www.facebook.com/bluejaysvisions/

Elizabeth James Perry
https://www.elizabethjamesperry.com/

Jonathan James Perry
https://www.jonathanjamesperry.com/

Robert Peters
https://xeepuuaee.wixsite.com/robert-peters-art/thirteen-moons

Annawon Weeden
https://firstlightfashion.square.site/

Jason Widdiss
www.etsy.com/shop/JasonWiddissWampum

71. Earrings of purple wampum by Marcus Hendricks (Photo courtesy of Wampanoag Shells)

TOP

72. Julia Marden with her museum quality pieces
(Photo courtesy of the artist)

BOTTOM:

73. Twined Quiver by Julia Marden
(Photo courtesy of Wampanoag Trading Post, and the artist)

74a. and b. A *Nush Wetu* exterior
(Photo courtesy of Institute for American Indian Studies, Jamie Robinson)

74b.
(Photo courtesy of Institute for American Indian Studies, Jamie Robinson)

TOP LEFT:
76. Interior *Turtle Wetu* (Photo by Lee Roscoe)

TOP RIGHT:
77. Interior *Nush Wetu*
(Photo courtesy of Institute for American Indian Studies, Jamie Robinson)

BOTTOM:
78. Interior *Nush Wetu*
(Photo by Sean Gibbons, courtesy of Plimoth Patuxet Museums)

79. Interior *Nush Wetu* (Photo by Sean Gibbons, courtesy of Plimoth Patuxet Museums)

The Author

As a longtime Massachusetts journalist, environmental educator and activist, with a decades-long interest in Indigenous and Wampanoag culture and history, Lee Roscoe has written frequently about the Wampanoag. She organized a drive in favor of federal recognition for the Mashpee Wampanoag, and helped save hundreds of acres of land in part sacred to the tribe. Roscoe is the Cape Cod correspondent for *Artscope* magazine, the author of *Wrap Yourself a Designer Dress*, based on her pioneering multi-use fashions, and of *Dreaming Monomoy's Past, Walking its Present*; *a subjective and objective account of the interacting nature and culture of a typical coastal area.* Roscoe is also an award-winning playwright whose work is often supported by the Massachusetts Cultural Council. For more see: www.artistsandmusicians.org/writers_corner/leeroscoe.html

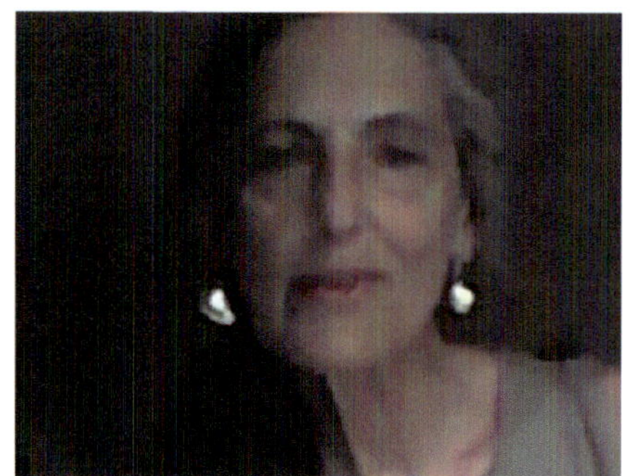